BeFIT 4 BETTER HEALTH

Master Your Health & Fitness

Transformation

Dr. Maude Exantus, DNP

Master Your Health and Fitness Transformation

By Dr. Maud Exantus, DNP, Certified Health Coach, IFBB Pro Athlete

Published by Nurse Empowerment & Leadership Publishing

18510 Pines Blvd, Pembroke Pines, Florida 33029.

This book or parts thereof may not be reproduced in any form, stored in retrieval system or transmitted in any form by means of electronic, mechanical, photocopy, recording, texting, or otherwise without prior written permission of the author, except as provided by United States of America Copyright law. Inquiries about the book should be directed to :

info@befit4betterhealth.com

All RIGHTS RESERVED ISBN :

Printed in The United States of America

Dedication

This book is dedicated to my mother, Marlene Sateigne, whose love and support sustained me throughout my life. She raised me in becoming a strong woman of God filled with faith and God's perfect love. Who gave me the courage to overcome difficult and challenging moments in achieving my dreams.

Table of Contents

Introduction: BeFit for Better Health --------------------------------- 1

CHAPTER ONE: Journey into Fitness ----------------------------- 5

CHAPTER TWO: Defining Health & Fitness --------------------- 16

CHAPTER THREE: Trusting the Process ------------------------ 30

CHAPTER FOUR: The Fit Lifestyle -------------------------------- 38

CHAPTER FI: Nutrition -- 50

CHAPTER SIX: Get Fit with Health Coaching -------------------- 72

CHAPTER SEVEN: Creating Your Training Plan ---------------- 79

CONCLUSION --- 93

About the Author --- 96

Introduction

BeFit for Better Health

In the past few years, the health of many people is progressively getting worse. A healthy and physically active life has shown to benefit people in living in the ailment of being healthy, both physically and mentally. This book inspires to motivate individuals to increase regular exercise and balance healthy nutrition meal portions. I hope this book will help you to set your health and fitness goals, and jump-start your fitness journey for better health. The journey to achieving a physical fitness transformation, and maintaining a healthy weight can be challenging.

As a professional figure bodybuilder athlete, full-time nurse practitioner working countless hours and attended graduate school for my doctor degree education, while competing in bodybuilding, shows the journey wasn't always comfortable achieving my personal fitness goals. I understand everyone does not have the same goals to train for a bodybuilding competition. I have learned throughout my fitness journey from personal trainers, nutrition coaches, and health and fitness education courses that a discipline and consistent habits of balanced nutrition and weight training can help an individual achieve a healthy and fit lifestyle.

Health and fitness have a major significance in the life of everyone. There's nothing more important than health, and maintaining an optimal functional physical fitness level for anyone's fitness conditions. Healthy and fit people can enjoy life very happily and peacefully. You have heard the saying that "Health is Wealth." to maintain good health, we need to take care of our overall well being correctly. We have to eat healthily, sleep, exercise, and manage our mental stress levels. Together with healthy food and physical activities, we need to balance and transform our spiritual and mental well-being to experience a physical transformation. Improving our physical and mental fitness is very important for a person to be successful and to do one's best in society.

Now, to get fit, you must decide to start. Sometimes, we tend to overthink the process of getting started. Don't wait or overthink about getting into the best shape of your life. Just start by making the commitment, then develop the discipline and consistency along the journey to see the results you desire. I am incredibly grateful to have worked with some amazing coaches over the years to help with my fitness and health transformation. The journey of developing my personal fitness goals was filled with many challenges, disappointments, and sometimes depression. I have learned that with sound coaching support and hard work, you can arrive at your goals too. Once you have achieved your goals, it becomes your responsibility to continue the journey in mastering your health and fitness transformation for better health. The lessons and experience in this book will place you in control of your health and keep you motivated to take ownership and master your fitness transformation for life.

What I know for sure is this; fitness is genuinely about empowering others to understand they are the master creator for transforming their health and fitness lifestyle. I hope this book will help you overcome all your health struggles and empower you in pursuit of your health and fitness goals. Living a healthy and vibrant life is the pathway for better health. Go ahead today; make the decision to start your health and fitness journey by reading the pages within this book. Let the power within you spark the motivation that will guide you to take ownership of your self-care, which will produce longevity for better health.

BeFit 4 Better Health mission focuses on inspiring and influencing the culture of healthcare to intergrade an increasing amount of consistent physical fitness activity, health coaching, and education strategies for healthy lifestyle modification that will improve healthcare. With hope in leading to improve the health and well being of many people in living an active and vibrant life.

CHAPTER ONE

Journey into Fitness

"The strongest light is the light that shines within you. Use it to lead the way of your life."

I want to share my story with you in hopes to give you the motivation and encouragement to live your best healthy life now, in your own unique way. My story begins as a young girl born in Port Au Prince, Haiti, where the culture value of earning an education and strength is symbolic for ultimate survival and must in every household. My mother migrated to the United Stated years ago with hopes in her heart at an early age to embark on the journey called the "American Dream" for her seven children's success. As a child, the journey wasn't always easy, with limited resources and support. Growing up, I watched my father abuse my mother to the point of death; then, my father abandoned me. My father's abusive behaviors towards my mother brought many painful emotions clouded with depression, fear, and anxiety for years into my life. Growing up, I often felt neglected and abandoned by my father's absence. I struggled through high school with depression and aggressive behaviors towards others.

My father's rejection and abandonment left me feeling hopeless, searching to find love in different places for years. I watched my mother struggle as a single parent without support living in America, struggling to make ends meet every day. I never allowed my circumstances to define my life. I had a determined mindset with laser-like precision to achieve that dream and make my mother proud. I understood the sacrifices my mother made for her children.

The challenges in my childhood years resulted in various stressful moments and academic challenges in high school. I still managed to push through with tenacity and extreme hard work to study and finish high school along with completing a rigorous Licensed Practical Nursing vocational program while in high school. I am extremely grateful for having teachers, such as Mrs.

Emma Lee, Mrs. Elmore, and many other great teachers and leaders on my path. Their consistent support was a major factor in my academic success, along with my mother's sacrifices. Through God's grace, I never gave up on education, even in the most difficult moments. I always knew for sure, I had a passion to care and love people. Graduating from high school and earning a Florida board LPN nursing license at 18 years old, right after high school was the best rewarding experience to starting living my dream caring and nurturing people back to health. Education was my only hope for unlocking poverty and access to my dreams. I continued to pursue an education in nursing with the same drive, passion, and determination that was evident in my mother sacrifices for freedom and living the American Dream. I continued later in college in becoming a Registered Nurse, Nurse Practitioner, and earning a Doctor in Nursing Practice degree. I am blessed and incredibly proud of my accomplishments and achievements while confronting overwhelming adversity.

Despite dealing with emotional neglect, rejection, and depression, fitness was another path that helped with overcoming the dark moments. Through my struggles, I found strength and pathways for success through fitness and personal spiritual relationship God with faith. Through all the traumatic disappointments, I was always physically active and spiritually ground through the church community, that provided an outlet to overcome the dark clouds of depressions.

A few months after graduating high school, my physical active lifestyle decreased along with unhealthy eating habits. I began to experience an increase in weight gain, abnormal menstrual cycles, and increasing symptoms of fatigue worsening with time. I tried to make small adjustments with modifying nutrition habits a little on my own but I wasn't consistent. The symptoms were getting worst, I continued working long hours shifts as a LPN nurse and making no time to take care of myself. I decided to visit my primary care physician months later for a physical exam, abdominal ultrasound, and laboratory blood evaluation. To receive the worst news from my physician, I was diagnosed with Polycystic Ovarian Syndrome (PCOS). This condition affects woman's hormone levels to be imbalance, causing problems with female fertility, cardiac function, appearances, weight gain, and abnormal cycles of high insulin levels and insulin resistance.

The symptoms of Polycystic Ovarian Syndrome (PCOS) were the causes of the steadily extra weight gain, irregular menses, fatigue, and imbalance hormones. This information about my health changed my perspective about making the appropriate changes with exercising and nutrition for better health. My doctor started me on birth control pills to help regulate my menses (period). After months of taking birth control pills, I continue to feel tired with chronic lower energy, and nothing was working. I was feeling worse, and my doctor was considering starting another medication called Metformin to manage my health conditions.

This diagnosis was the catalyst that placed me on the path again to an active fit lifestyle that lead into bodybuilding and mastering my own personal health and fitness transformation. I invested into hiring a personal trainer, nutrition coach, and adjusted my personal lifestyle to fit into my health and fitness goals. I began weight training regularly with my trainer, Luc Neree, to maintain a healthy weight and manage my PCOS symptoms. Luc was my favorite trainer. During that time, I exercised and weight trained regularly 4-5 days per week to maintain an active life and healthy weight. After 3-6 months of consistent hard training, my symptoms of PCOS began to change, dropped 20lbs from baseline weight within 12 weeks, body fat percent decreased from 28% percent to 20% from baseline body fat percent. In the process, my menstrual cycle and hormones levels returned back to normal. Gradually, within six months of training and dieting, my symptoms of PCOS resolved, and my period was regular. I was off my birth control medication that was prescribed to regulate my hormones. Hallelujah!!!

However, the journey continued for months with my trainer, and occasionally I would experience relapse back into unhealthy eating habits. Training with Luc Neree provided support for maintaining and getting involve in other physical activities such as running marathons. That's how my addiction for running long distances all started. I began to enjoy exercising again no matter what issues that were happening, including dealing with depression and anxiety. Exercises with weight training and nutrition was the best medicine for my body. Through it, exercising kept me mentally balanced and focused. I always felt the strongest and most powerful in the gym. During my training time, exercise had always given me a sense of empowerment and brought balance to my life. I searched for various ways to continue challenging my fitness potentials. I decided to even join a Crossfit gym for three years to maximize and develop my fitness goals in small group fitness settings. Training in group fitness environments and partner training were great methods, which kept me motivated on track with my personal health and fitness goals.

My consistent training with Luc and Crossfit training began to inspire people. My nurse colleague, Maggie Payne, consistently kept telling me over time, I was beginning to look like a perfect professional fitness model on a magazine cover. At the time, I was clueless about what she was expressing to me. People were seeing the changes happening and amazed at my transformation results. My fitness goals were only focused on maintaining my health and being depression-free without being placed on antidepressants. My personal health and fitness transformation brought many people on my path encouraging me to compete in bodybuilding shows. Then, a year later, I found a fitness coach that introduced me into the world of bodybuilding competitions.

The journey of competing in bodybuilding on the amateur stage, and becoming a professional figure bodybuilding athlete, and earning an IFBB pro card was filled with many obstacles. Many wins and some lost, but deep down inside, I believed that obtaining a pro card was an enormous goal to accomplish. I am grateful for my Coaches Hassan, and Stephanie. They truly changed my passion and love for bodybuilding. Coach Hassan and Stephanie's online training and nutrition program always kept me on track all-year-round for maintaining physical conditioning and fit physique. Through their online coaching services, they have given me one hundred percent of their time and energy. I never felt intimidated and uncomfortable with their program. I am incredibly grateful for having great fitness and nutrition Coaches such as Stephanie and Hassan; they are real role models coaches who are genuinely compassionate about coaching people for healthier lifestyle.

My passion and love for health and fitness along with my patients' influence in the clinics were the reasons that inspired me in becoming a health and fitness coach. Without a doubt, bodybuilding has aslo taught me many great lessons and experiences with physical, mental, and spiritual transformation. I have translated those discipline and consistency habits into my personal life. I consistently train and maintain an active lifestyle year-round. Lifting weights and healthy eating habits has become an acceptable way of embracing my body, and maintaining a healthy fit lifestyle. There is nothing wrong with lifting heavy and being strong. It is acceptable for women to be physically fit, strong, and beautiful with grace.

The journey on the path to fitness, health, nutrition, and bodybuilding has undoubtedly helped me to value my self-worth and develop a healthier spiritual outlook on life. Mastering my fitness journey has allowed me to develop the discipline, consistency, and commitment for better health. I used to only care about the numbers on the scale, letting weight motivate me rather than how healthy I felt. I used to diet to lose weight on the scale or for unrealistic images and exercised to burn calories rather than eating calories for muscle and burning fat. The best thing that happened to me was transforming my life for better health. It has truly blessed me with learning how to be disciplined, especially with my nutrition and building my body and remaining in the best physical shape. The journey and transformation allowed me to appreciate my muscular body and femininity.

Being a woman with muscle was challenging to accept at the beginning of my fitness transformation. The personal myths and opinions from others used to block me from appreciating my beauty. We live in a society were women with muscles, and fit bodies are referred to as being manly or bulky because they have robust and sexy curves. For many years, I walked around, hitting from the shame of people, especially fearing women that would call me names. These myths and opinions hindered me from lifting and building my body. Since I started competing, I was shocked by the number of people that approach me every day, asking questions about my physique and often received positive feedback, especially from men and women. Sometimes, even men were inspired by my results. Bodybuilding has given me back my self-confidence and helped me overcome much insecurity.

My health and fitness transformation journey has changed my life. What evolved from that experience and came afterward impacted my life in many ways. The journey has led me into becoming the best version of myself and inspiring many to be fit for better health. I recognize myself as an extremely "fit" person mentally and spiritually; that's consistent and committed to exercising, with healthy nutrition habits, and emotionally and mentally strong. These traits changed my name in becoming "MaudyFit" I had to overcome many struggles and sacrifices in maintaining great physical fitness to produce mental and spiritual fitness. When you are thriving in these areas, a person can become "fit" for better health.

Everything I have learned from my coaches and trainers has taught me how to maintain a disciplined life with a healthy behavior pattern committed to obtaining and maintaining a fit body. Competing and fitness have certainly changed my life for better health, so this health and fitness journey has all become more than just a hobby. Lifting weights has become a way of life. There is nothing wrong with lifting heavyweight and being strong. You have heard my story, and now, it's your turn to create your path to master your health and fitness transformation. You can accomplish anything you want in life. It all starts with you making your health and fitness goals a priority. Be willing to commit, discipline yourself, and remain consistent with your health, training, and nutrition habits. Now, it's time to challenge yourself and find the courage to train your butt off to master your health and fitness transformation. I hope you'll make a decision to overcome your challenges and learn about various ways you can achieve and master your health and fitness goals.

Although my life was filled with challenges, God used those experiences to direct my path into brighter pathways to support many in their own health and fitness journey. Starting your fitness and health journey requires tenacity driven through motivation. When things get tough, you must build the courage and strength to work through the struggles. The victory in your health and fitness transformation resides within you to produce the desired results you seek daily to manifest.

CHAPTER TWO

Defining Health & Fitness

"Exercise is the Best Medicine"

How do you define fitness? Achieving great fitness conditioning is built on a foundation of being self-disciplined, committed, and consistent. Physical fitness can be defined by how active a person is daily, base on their cardio, strength, and flexibility condition. Being physically fit allows your body to complete daily functional task, appear in our best, increases our mental awareness, and keeps you in the best overall health. Unfortunately, being physically fit is not a one size fit process. Just like everyone have different body types, lifestyle circumstances, and goals. Therefore, fitness levels, meal plans, supplements, and weight training exercises will ultimately be different to produce great results.

Fitness levels can be measured in many ways and vary from person to person. To have optimal physical fitness, it is essential for a person to maintain a balance overall production level in every part of the fitness zones with cardio, strength, and flexibility evenly. For example, when someone works out by only doing resistant weights and refuses to work on improving cardio, flexibility, and recovery, they may look healthy and robust, but they are not truly fit. Someone may work out by doing cardio only for weight loss but does not include various weight training and flexibility, lose weight, and look good. Still, it doesn't mean you are healthy and fit. Take sometime and review the five different elements of physical fitness.

Five Different Elements of Physical Fitness

1. Aerobic or cardiovascular endurance- the body's ability to circulate blood to deliver and use oxygen effectively.

2. Muscular strength- the amount of force muscles can generate against resistance.

3. Muscular endurance- the ability for the muscle to

withstand repeated contractions or forces over a set period.

4. Flexibility-the full range of motion available to joints and muscles.

5. Body composition- is measurements for a persons' overall fitness status.

These elements can be specific for assessing overall fitness levels for improving lean body mass, including muscles, bone tissue, organs, and compared to body fat. The goal of physical fitness will help increase lean body mass and decrease body fat.

Throughout my professional fitness experiences, I have learned most people do not understand the science behind exercise and nutrition. They are plenty of different media information available on healthy ways to eat, and the information does not always explain the details to people on how to master personal fitness transformations. They're also many fitness myths circulating. It's critical to understand the basics about managing good fitness programs and Marco nutrients such as carb, fats, and proteins to promote fat loss and increase muscles. I will cover a little more on macros in the next chapters. Some of these health and fitness information can be particularly harmful to your health, and increase the risk of physical injury without results or improvement in overall fitness goals.

What does health mean to you? There are many definitions and various ideas of what the word "health" truly means. The World Health Organization defines health as- "a state of complete physical, mental and social well-being and not merely the absence of disease or infirmity." My definition of health can be defined as not just a physical state, but also mental, spiritual, and even nutritional state of well-being. Health overall, cannot be combined into one category as there are different avenues of health. For example, your physical health is the health of your physical body, leaving out your mental, spiritual, and nutritional needs. When you think about your physical health, that is defining the actual shape and the physical condition. Think about it? Someone may suffer from physical abnormalities such as trouble breathing, high blood pressure, and low or high heart rate. Physical health is something that you can see, such as test results from an x-ray, blood work, physical performance levels, and other outcomes.

An essential aspect of health is not only the physical but the mental health of an individual as well. The mind is a powerful thing, capable of producing feelings and emotions that can truly impact a person's overall health. Exercising has shown to improve mental focus along with mood. Current evidence in the literature says that regular exercise can help keep your brain sharp by improving your focus and concentration. Some studies have even shown that exercising can decrease the chance of Alzheimer's disease and other mental health issues. Even low impact exercises, walking, and using your body weight for strength training can help with boosting your mood and give a person uplifting feelings.

There are different shreds of evidence out there showing that regular fitness exercise is one of the essential things a person can do to improve physical and mental health and prevent diseases. Taking the time to invest 30-60 minutes to exercise 3-5 days per week can make the heart stronger and develop more efficient muscles. When you exercise, you are delivering oxygen and nutrients into your body. This improves the functions of your cardiovascular system resulting in more energy and health. These behaviors can reduce excess body fat and decrease the chances of having a heart attack. Doing low impact activity can even help your body by improving your good cholesterol and lowering your blood pressure.

Prevention Health is Better than Treatment

Maintaining an optimal level of health and fitness levels is essential for living a higher quality of life. Health is light for life, family, and community. Your health matters because everything we do relates to our well-being. Our well-being directly affects our actions and emotions. Therefore, it is essential for everyone to achieve some form of fitness capacity to subdue stress, reduce the risk of illness, and ensure positive well being. Every day, we should strive to learn how to add more value to our spiritual, emotional, mental, and physical needs. Every time you step into the gym, make adjustments in our nutrition habits, or take time to exercise, you are placing yourself in control of your health in preventing chronic diseases. Becoming the best vision of you requires taking ownership of your health, fitness, and wellness.

I have learned that during the whole process of my fitness journey has allowed for a more in-depth search within and seeking insight for maintaining physical and spiritual guidance for health for life. You can start your path by creating a plan that's going to make you happy and feasible to your lifestyle. I have learned that making the journey fun and memorable will allow you to enjoy exercising training. I usually don't like waking up early at 4:00 am to do my cardio expect long runs with friends once a week on the weekend. Training with others in groups or gym partners makes exercising enjoyable. You have to make training and fitness fun and a way of life to reach your goals.

Benefits of Exercise

We have all heard it many times before that regular exercise is good for you, and it can help you lose weight. But if you are like many individuals, you are either too busy, you have a sedentary job, or you haven't yet changed your exercise habits. To get the most benefit from exercising, you should try to get the recommended amount of exercise daily to maintain great health. If you can do it, the payoff investment is that you will feel better, help prevent or control many diseases, and likely even live longer.

Everyone can benefit from physical activity. For most people, it is possible to begin exercising on your own at a slow pace. If you have never exercised before, start with 10 minutes of light exercise. A brisk walk every day is a good first exercise. Slowly increase how hard you exercise and for how long. Talk to your doctor before starting an exercise program. Remember, if your doctor or practitioner is already monitoring you for a health problem, such as heart disease or osteoarthritis, your doctor or practitioner can work with a trainer and health coach to help you find other exercises to improve your overall health. Regular physical activities and routine practice, are vital for people of all age groups, especially younger and middle age older generations. Health and fitness bring happiness in life and helps a person to live a stress-free and disease-free life.

BeFit 4 Better Health Fitness Steps

Step # 1 Get started with your fitness and health goals

Sometimes, the hardest step is getting started. Start with having a clear mindset, balancing your spiritual self, set goals, develop a plan, meal plan, have fun, and enjoy running a clear mind and feeling good about your journey. Then, commit and develop the discipline in finding balance in your life to switch into a healthy mode that will have lasting results in lifestyle changes. Developing a consistent plan, educate yourself, and connect with your fitness goals. Invest in a personal trainer and coach that can assist you with health and fitness progress.

Step # 2 Get going with the journey to fitness and better health

What's your motivation? We work hard to gain wealth and own material things. How often do we work hard towards achieving ownership of our health? Think exercise and nutrition like cash. Every day of working out is like putting money away towards owning our health or being in control of our health. The less you invest in the process, the less you can expect from your health and body. You can't expect healthy outcomes if you're not doing anything right now. Don't expect your body to function well forever if you are not doing anything now to allow it to function effectively. What's your motivating factor? Obstacles will come; don't wait, put your plans into action with small goals then build on these goals. Start with exercising one day per week, then two days, then 3-5 days per week.

Step # 3 Maintain the momentum towards an optimal level of health

To maintain one's health and fitness, it is important that you eat healthily and exercise consistently. With small adjustments, anyone can sustain a healthy lifestyle. These adjustments can include a change in diet or a well-planned exercise routine. When you exercise, it is important to know what you are affecting. The right fitness coach can help you develop an exercise program designed to improve and maintain your overall fitness performance. The more frequent you can exercise your results can decreased risk of cardiovascular disease, type 2 diabetes, depression, some cancers, and anxiety. Many people fail to achieve the recommended exercise levels.

I certainly believe the culture of healthcare needs to be shifted by increasing consultations services for exercise and nutrition counseling. I remember three years ago working for Humana

Healthcare completing health assessments screenings. I used fifteen minutes to discuss physical activity, nutrition, and weight training exercises with my patients and provide them with resources to encourage them with weekly events and referred them to trained exercise professionals. I remember within six to ten weeks, my patients were reaching back out to share their successful results and experiences within their health. These consistent calls and testimonies were motivating factors that stimulate my passion in developing the knowledge for physical fitness training and health coaching. In the next few pages, you'll successful key points usually shared with my patients and clients to help jump-start their own fitness journey.

BeFit 4 Better Health Key for Success

Benefits of Physical Activity Key Points:

1. Healthy people achieve and maintain a healthy weight

2. Reduces feelings of stress, anxiety & depression

3. Builds and maintains healthy bones, muscles & joints

4. Boosts energy level through relaxation daily

5. Improves quality of sleep aim for 7-8 hours per night

6. Physical activity reduces the risk of you:

7. Dying from heart disease or stroke

8. Developing high blood pressure, cholesterol & diabetes

9. Developing obesity

10. Developing osteoporosis – exercise builds strong bones & muscles

Importance of Health and Fitness

Health and fitness are very important for people who want to live a healthy life very happily and peacefully. A healthy and fit person is only capable of living life to its fullest extent. We can say a person is healthy and fit if he/she is physically and mentally fit. Physically and mentally fit people become less prone to medical conditions. Health and fitness of any person help in:

1. Decreasing the risk of diseases such as (high blood pressure, diabetes, coronary heart diseases, colon cancer, osteoporosis, obesity, stroke, breast cancer, etc.)

2. Make you feel better, both physically and mentally.

3. Improving confidence level with everything within your life.

4. Heals injuries soon and builds a strong immune system.

5. It helps to live longer by adding years to your life.

6. Reduces stress and improves the quality of life.

7. Reducing anxiety level, stress, and feelings of depression.

Become Active for Better Health

Exercising and consistently working on your fitness goals is an integral part of a healthy lifestyle. Exercise prevents health problems, builds strength, boosts energy, and can help you reduce stress. It can also help you maintain healthy body weight and curb your appetite. These habits can create paths to improve your health. The Department of Health and Human Services recommends one of the following activity levels for adult fitness and health benefits:

1. Seventy five minutes of vigorous aerobic activity weekly plus muscle-strengthening activities two or more days a week.

2. One hundred and fifty minutes of moderate aerobic activity weekly plus muscle-strengthening activities two or more days a week. Break down to 30 minutes of training 5 days weekly

3. An equivalent mix of moderate and vigorous aerobic activity plus muscle-strengthening activities for two or more days a week.

Moderate aerobic activity examples include:

1. Walking fast
2. Water aerobics
3. Bicycling on mostly level ground
4. Pushing a lawnmower

Vigorous aerobic activity includes:

1. Running
2. Swimming laps
3. Fast bicycling or biking hills
4. Playing basketball or soccer
5. Playing singles tennis

Muscle-strengthening exercises include:

1. Lifting weights or using resistance bands

2. Calisthenics that use body weight for resistance

3. Heavy gardening or yard work

CHAPTER THREE

Trusting the Process

"We become what we want to be by consistently being what we want to become each day"- Richard G. Scott

The beginning of my fitness journey was filled with disappointing moments in the process, especially with developing my overall fitness and physique, especially in developing the gluteus maximums muscles along with conditioning my legs. Sometimes, results didn't often come immediately as expected. I learned through the process that it takes time, patient, and consistency with showing up to put in the work into exercising training to see the results you desire. I wish someone had educated me about the fitness journey. Many years ago, I remembered listening to the myths about these quick-fix results and lifting weights. As a result, I was often disappointed with the process. This resulted in not being motivated to push myself beyond my potential because I lacked trust in the process.

It has shown that it takes about four weeks for a person to begin seeing the body change, eight weeks for friends to see it, but twelve weeks for the rest of the world and others to start seeing your transformation. Depending on the person, this can even take six months process. The bottom line, you must learn the arts of being patient on your fitness journey. Being patient allows you to embrace the journey and become more confident within your skin. Everything is possible; the process takes hard work, discipline, and commitment to building that sculptured healthy physique.

Most people never realize the importance of being healthy and fit. They generally underestimate the importance of good health and physical activity, as they never know how completely they perform and train their bodies. We all know that health is wealth, but research has shown only a few people follow consistent physical active healthy habits. Being healthy and fit helps us in carrying out our daily tasks. Being healthy does not only free the body of diseases, but it also means to have a tensionless mind. If a person has an unhealthy mind, he cannot have an healthy body. Good health from both body and mind helps us to get success in life and enjoy it to the full extent. Good mental health and physical health is the foundation of well-being. A healthy body gives us physical strength and confidence. Good physical health helps us in our troubled times, whereas poor physical health becomes weaker and prone to diseases.

Doing any physical activity is better than doing none. If you currently do no physical activity, start by doing some, and gradually build-up to the recommended amount. Be active on most, preferably all days every week, so you can master your health and fitness transforming changes. One of my BeFit for Better Health concepts uses an acronym called LIGHT for people on the pathway to transforming into their health and fitness goals. Living a life filled with great health allows you to "Let Your Light Shine" with a commitment to maintaining great overall health and fitness status.

L.I.G.H.T.

L –Live a vibrant, healthy, and fit lifestyle you desire through sound discipline, consistency, and commitment towards successful health results.

I –Initiate an action focus goals to inspire and motivate you to enjoy a newfound confidence and delight in the simplicity of radiant health.

G – Grow and develop flexible, healthy behaviors consisting of a healthy and fit lifestyle.

H –Holistically nourish you, family, and friends with improving health behaviors, fitness, and overall wellness. Connect with your mind, spirit, and body in improving your health for success.

T –Transform your life through personal self-care, by taking ownership of your nutrition habits, health, and exercise-training methods to assist you with your health and wellness goals. Then use your personal transformation results to empower your family, friends, and community.

How to Maintain Health and Fitness

There are various ways you can maintain healthy and fit habits if you regularly follow the following:

You should regularly get involve in daily physical exercises by getting some time off from our much hectic schedule; 30 to 60 minutes of exercise daily or five to six times a week is ideal for anybody to remain fit. A good goal is to exercise 3-5 times a week for at least 30 minutes each time. However, most people need to start with three days, then gradually increase to 4-5 days per week. Start by exercising 2 or 3 times a week for 30 minutes at a time. Once you feel comfortable, slowly increase the amount of time and the number of days a week that you exercise.

Healthy and clean food in the right amount and at the right time is very necessary for a person to stay healthy and fit. Healthy nutrition with high-fiber, low-fat, high protein, and a rich source of vitamins and minerals is the key to good health.

To get fit and healthy, a good sleeping pattern is very necessary for any person. We need to maintain discipline in our daily routine and focus on good sleeping patterns, which must start and end at the right time. Taking a quality sleep of eight hours each night boosts our immune system and helps in preventing cardiovascular diseases as well as improves mood. An inadequate sleeping pattern can lead to sleep disorders and various mental disorders.

Monitor Your Progress

It's important you find a way to monitor your progress. Keeping track of your progress will help with trusting the process and improving your health and fitness goals. Take the same measurements about six weeks after you begin an exercise program and periodically afterward. I usually recommend staying away from the scale. I usually use an online fitness app from my coaches to help keep my focus on track with my fitness goals. I usually tell people once you hit a particular milestone, enjoy the journey, celebrate those small victories and moments Each time you repeat your assessment, celebrate your progress, and adjust your fitness goals accordingly with coach or trainer. Share your results with even your doctor or practitioner, and health coach for additional guidance. These simple recommendations will make a significant difference in helping you get through the process.

Five Key Important Steps for Physical Transformation

1. Start the process: It doesn't matter where you are in your fitness level. Sometimes, starting the process can be the most challenging thing to do. You have to start somewhere. I recommend you start with small tasks, then building up. You have the option of investing in a personal trainer or health coach for support and guidance.

2. Commit to the process: Don't just get started, but you have to make a commitment to follow through on your

goals. People often asked how I managed to maintain physique year-round. Some say its great genetics and luck. Truth be told, it is all about putting in the time to build my body and training, nutrition, and actively putting in the work to making a dream become a reality.

3. Do the work in the process: You can't just set goals and expect everything to work out in your favor. You have to be willing to do the work. I usually will put in the 2-5 hours a day to build my body for exercise, meal prep nutrition, and practice posing routines for competitions. You have to actively work on making your health and fitness goals a reality.

4. Trust the process: you have heard success is a process. It doesn't happen overnight. I had to learn how to take my time and pace myself. Rome wasn't built in one day. As much as we would like to have a step-by-step roadmap for getting to our destination, results don't always come that way.

5. Don't give up on the process. You have to believe in your goals for what you are trying to achieve. Don't focus on where you are or where you've been. That's why I have always made it a point to write down my goals. It's my

way of staying focus on personal health and fitness transformation. I am naturally a passionate endurance/cardio athlete. My training programs include high volume weight training and plyometrics, especially for my legs. I have learned through completing fitness training; it takes a lot of dedication, discipline, and determination to reach any fitness goals. I remember there was a time I wanted to give up on lifting weights because I thought I would never arrive at my personal fitness goals. My bodybuilding prep for competition training has taught me that it takes patience and a lot of hard work to increase muscle mass and tone. Everyone has what it takes to burn fat and build muscles, but requires hard work with accomplishing those goals. You have to be willing to trust the process and not give up at every moment on the journey.

CHAPTER FOUR

The Fit Lifestyle

'Motivation is what gets you started. Habit is what keeps you going." - Jim Ryun

Being physically fit and healthy is based on a lifestyle committed to physical fitness. There's a popular proverb that states, "To whom much is given, much will be required." You have to live up to your fitness lifestyle and set positives examples for your community, colleagues, and family. As a professional figure bodybuilder athlete with five years plus experiences in physical training in the gym and track runner. The exhilaration for fitness has taught me how to develop consistent success in becoming the best version of myself for my overall fitness development. I have learned physical fitness transformation doesn't happen overnight or a few weeks; instead, it requires commitment towards working hard and overcoming challenges that will lead to successful outcomes on your health.

A few things to keep in mind in pursuit of your fitness goals are to keep things "Simple and Sustainable" it is about the quality of your physical training (form, intensity, efforts) and remaining consistent with the goals. Also, "Train with PURPOSE" train for performance and not results for the scale, that is such a better perspective to maintaining a healthy fit lifestyle. Once you start a new fitness program, our human nature can go into autopilot for the most part after a couple of days or weeks into our training. Sometimes, we need to evaluate our situation, goals, and reasoning as to WHY we are doing what we are doing and what for. I have learned to go to the gym to train, run, and walk on the park with a purpose, will allow us to stay crystal clear and focused on our goals.

I believe some people have called me a fitness fanatic. I actually enjoy working out; I also love nutrition and food period! —the majority of the time, anyway. I don't always evaluate fitness and health as all about the outer appearance. Of course, presenting a fit body is a major component in ones' overall well being, more so mentally, but being healthy and fit doubtlessly is also about the mind, the external body, and the internal body.

However, living a fit lifestyle has many important health benefits. You can start with free weight exercises, including bodyweight squats, walking, and cycling. In fact, these movements have positive improvements in joint-degrading diseases such as rheumatoid arthritis and osteoarthritis. People who suffer from arthritis have chronic inflammation of the joints, whereas wear-and-tear of the ligaments causes osteoarthritis. Strength training has shown to improve joint health and function.

Unfortunately, women typically choose not to strength train or lift weights, as they fear becoming "too bulky" or "manly looking." The appearance of female bodybuilders typically causes this fear as they, like male bodybuilders, strive to have muscular, virtually fat-free bodies. However, the hormone results of natural women prevent them from having the same musculature appearance as men. The male sex hormone, testosterone, has anabolic effects on muscle/strength. Nevertheless, men can also benefit consistent strength training with nutrition to increase mass and strength training, has been proven to increase joint strength and muscle functions, and to be a safe and viable physical activity for women and men.

There are many benefits that maintain peak fitness levels range from increased muscle size and strength, increased bone mineral density, increased cardiovascular to higher self-esteem, improved self-image, increased confidence, and even increased libido. It has shown that weightlifting training has one of the lowest injury rates compared to other major physical activity, meaning people can safely train with little risk and high rewarding results. With the increasingly sedentary lifestyle of many people with a busy lifestyle that most people live, it's a must to make an effort to stay healthy. As a result, everyone should utilize consistent cardio and weight training for strength, in order to have an optimal time and cost-efficient way to improve overall health and physical function.

Knowing your Fitness Level

It does matter where you are currently in your fitness journey, or whether you are just beginning your new fitness program or already in progress. Knowing your fitness level is very important in the process of exercising and achieving your health and fitness goals. I highly recommend you take the time to meet with a professional fitness trainer or even a health coach to assess your fitness level. As a result, your coach/trainer can help you begin training workout programs with exercises designed for your fitness level. There are many health and fitness coaching professional programs online or in your local area that can help you achieve your goals.

Before you consider starting any exercise program, first check with your primary health physician. If you're in good health with no chronic health problems, it's not always recommended to consult a physician or practitioner for medical clearance. The results of your fitness assessment can help you set goals for staying active and improving fitness outcomes. Then have a professional health coach or trainer completed an assessment to evaluate the five areas of fitness conditions. Measuring your fitness performance levels can be a multi-dimensional process; for example, a long-distance runners can have excellent cardiovascular health, but if all you do is running and cardio, you won't have a lot of strength or muscular tone. Its very important to maintain balance within all the different areas in your fitness training araes to improve your overall health. By the same measure, someone who is overweight and aerobically fit can be healthier than someone who is in the normal weight range but doesn't exercise. Therefore fitness is not always about your physical structure. Even though our society has placed emphasis on physical appearance. You should aim to focus on mental and physical conditioning. Indeed with time if you are consistent you will see lasting physical changes and health benefits.

PHASES OF FITNESS CONDITIONING

Often, physical fitness training programs are divided into three phases: preparatory, conditioning, and maintenance. The starting phases for different individuals vary depending on age, fitness levels, and previous physical activity.

PREPARATORY PHASE

The preparatory phase helps both the cardiorespiratory and muscular systems get used to exercising, preparing the body to handle the conditioning phase. In the preparatory phase for improving muscular endurance and strength through weight training, you should start easily and progress gradually. Try using lightweights the first week to learn the proper form for exercises. Lightweights will also help minimize muscle soreness and decrease the likelihood of injury to the muscles, joints, and ligaments. You should aim 15 to 20 repetitions x 3-4 sets per exercise.

CONDITIONING PHASE

The conditioning phase normally begins after three to six weeks of consistent training sometimes longer depending on the person. I recommend to be patient during these times. To reach the desired level of fitness, you must increase the amount of exercise and/or workout intensity as your strength and/or endurance increases. To improve cardiorespiratory endurance, for example, you must increase the length of intensity or time of cardio. Its recommended to train at least three times a week and take no more than two days between workouts. As long as you continue to progress and get stronger while doing the exercises, continue to challenge yourself daily and weekly. This will prevent you from stop making progress towards your fitness goals. Usually tabata or HIIT trainings are great methods to target intensity and increase burning more body fat. As training progresses, you may want to increase training days or time to help promote further increases in endurance, strength and/or muscle mass development.

MAINTENANCE PHASE

The maintenance phase sustains is the highest level of fitness achieved in the conditioning phase. The emphasis here is no longer on progression. A well-designed 45 to 60-minute workout (including warm-up and cool-down) at the right intensity three times a week is enough to maintain almost any appropriate level of physical fitness this phase. Once you reach this phase you have become master of health and fitness goals. Its important you remain consistent in stage because you can be prone to replase. Early in my fitness journey if you recall, I also experienced relapse within my fitness journey too. Remember you are always growing and developing into a better version of yourself. Be consistent and reach out to your fitness partner or coach to help keep you on track. A great coach understands and will help get back on track to maintain your goals.

Health and Fitness Habits for Success

You have heard people say that human beings are 'Creatures of Habit'. Indeed, habits are routines of behaviors that occur outside of conscious awareness. Many habits are helpful, in that they help you to manage your time, and complete important routines everyday tasks. Is your habits serving you with mastering your health and fitness transformation journey? Did you know that your habits determine your future! That future includes your overall health. The world is rapidly changing and the habits you create concerning your health and fitness lifestyle will determine what you might long for in life. Its critical to develop habits that are helpful and consistent with your health and fitness values to serve your life goals for success.

Training habits for success:

When training each workout should last about 30mins- 45 minutes or one hour, including a proper warm-up and cool-down. Sometimes training times will depend on your specific goals with your coach or trainer. If you are new to using weights, begin with a full-body routine, three days a week. Begin with a variety of compound exercises such as body weight squats, push ups, pull ups, dumbbell rows, dumbbell shoulder presses, chest press, and exercises for the core and arms. These exercises will produce great results when done correctly. I usually starts my client with these types of training before progessing to advance weight lifting exercises.

Nutrition habits for success:

Eating for muscle size is no different than eating for health; you just need more of everything. Eat a diet rich in vegetables and fruits, whole grains, healthy portion size carbohydrates, and at least 1.0 to 1.5 grams of protein/kg of body weight. Monitor your marcos nutrients through different apps; develop routine habits of detoxing your body from process foods, sugars, and high carbs diets. Learn about types of foods sensitivity for your specific body type. Develop a habit to drinking more water daily. If possible start incorporating intermittent fasting 3-5 times per week in your eating habits. Remember to always speak with your physician or practitioner before making changes.

Building a foundation for success:

Incorporate resistance training into your routine to build the foundation of strength, endurance, and integrity of your joints and structures. Remember to consider adding circuit training; this will provide both a muscular and aerobic training benefit. As you continue to build your routine and remember to remain consistent in the exercises. Use a moderate weight that you can lift with little discomfort.

Building muscles for success:

If you want to build lean muscle mass, tone body, improve your strength, and define your body, and don't know where to start? Then you are going to have to train smarter, not harder. It's going to require you to challenge the muscles to grow. This is the moment that you are going to start to see improvement in their overall fitness transformation. Many fitness studies have shown that the 12 to 15-repetition range helps build the greatest amount of muscle mass and produces the tone. Be sure to use a challenging weight that makes every last repetition moderately difficult.

Health & Fitness Action Plan

Developing a health fitness action is not an easy task. In the next few paragraphs, I am going to give you some sample steps to start your own action plan. Remember, if you have specific health problems, please check with your doctor before implementing a routine to boost your fitness goals. Once your doctor gives you the go-ahead, you have no more excuses. To improve your fitness level, take these important steps: Follow U.S. guidelines for the minimum amount of exercise. That means exercising at a moderate intensity level for at least 2.5 hours spread over most days each week. At least twice a week, supplement aerobic exercise with weight-bearing activities that target all major muscles.

No matter what activity you choose for getting fit, never compare your progress to someone else results. Do your set goals, and if you are out of shape and hate exercise, start low and go slow and do not compare yourself with others. Even if the same group of people walked at the same pace every morning, they would not all show the same fitness measure. Give your body time to recover; also, one preventive step you can take is checking your resting heart rate before getting out of bed every morning and making a chart so you can see a consistent but gradual decrease over time. If your resting heart rate begins to increase, you may be overdoing it. As you work on improving your fitness, take it slow and steady to avoid injury or burnout. Above all, remember that consistency is key — if you keep at it, your hard work will pay off. I normally have all my clients check their resting heart and understand their specific fitness zones for training.

CHAPTER FIVE

Nutrition

"Nutrition Is Key to Living Well"

Proper nutrition is one of the essential elements of being healthy and living a long life. People deal with food every day, and food has been a part of life since the beginning of society. What we eat becomes our diet, and our diet plays a major role in deciding how healthy we are and how well our body functions. Without proper diet, our body cannot carry out the functions it needs to perform. Most people have some common knowledge of what is good and what is bad for the human body to consume. Fruits, vegetables, nuts, and grains are some common items people think of when they think of healthy foods.

However, it is not enough just to know what foods are good for your body. It is also important to understand why certain foods are good for you and what they do to help the body function. Food is anything we consume, whether it is for taste or for nutritional value. The nutritional value of a food is the value the food gives to the body to function. To identify whether a portion of food has poor or good nutritional value, people use a nutrition facts chart. The labels on food packages can display the amount of fat, sugar, calories, fiber, carbohydrates, cholesterol, calories, and more.

For several years now, I have been a nutrition coach researching food impact on the human body. I really enjoyed this topic and feel that it is very important for people to invest time in researching nutrition information, but unfortunately, the average person won't understand what he or she may have or may not have been doing right that they are not seeing results for years. Nutrition plays s a major role in the result of every major transformation. Of course, everyone is different and has their own thoughts on how they want to lose weight. Most people think that cutting calories or cabs completely out from the diet is the key to losing weight when it really is not. What I have learned from my personal transformation and nutrition science education is that there is no need to cut out carbs from calories because calories are actually important when it comes to working out and at what times to eat them benefit a person as well.

FINDING A BALANCE

1. Calories in Food > Calories Used = Weight Gain

2. Calories in Food < Calories Used = Weight Loss

3. Calories in Food = Calories Used = Weight Control

FIND YOUR OWN BALANCE AND GOALS!!!

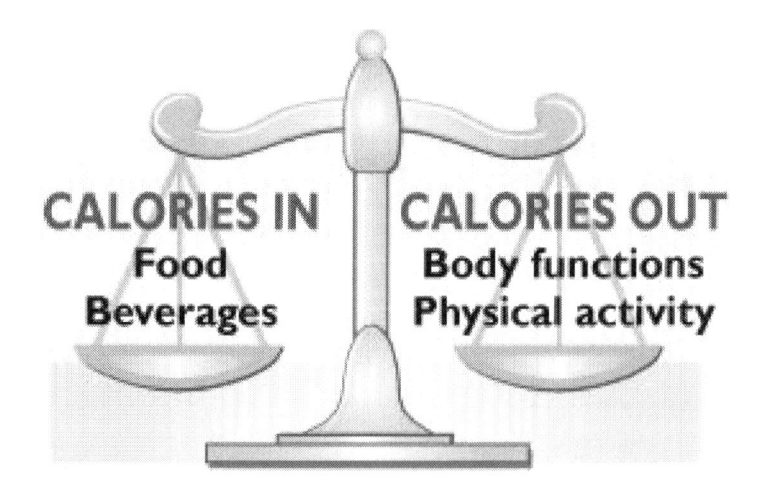

CALORIES IN
Food
Beverages

CALORIES OUT
Body functions
Physical activity

Overall to lose weight, you have to burn more than you eat. Base on the latest research, your body has to burn 3,500-calories per week to be in deficit to lose a pound of fat. Now think about it for a moment. How many calories is your body burning? This can be done through both diet and exercise, but the human body is complicated because everyone has different genetics and built differently. It's a bit of an oversimplification that you can choose to either burn your calories or reduce your intake. That's where the assistance of health and nutrition coaches can be beneficial to help you arrive at your goals.

It took me initially months to go through 12 months of consistent training and nutrition to make adjustments in my eating habits. Training and nutrition are critical to master your health and fitness transformation. I am 5-foot-6, I set a goal of being 145 pounds. This number on the scale was always frustrating, and I never considered what was truly healthy for my height and body. Even when I achieved it, my regimen was so strict about maintaining my results. My weight was constantly going up and down on the scale. I would someday eat whatever I wanted and not follow my coach's plans. You can't out-diet your training unless you can follow a consistent nutritious plan for your lifestyle; oftentimes, diet can fail you. I've learned the science of proper management of marcos from calories. Resulted in spending less hours on the treadmill to keep a lean body long term. I keep telling people all the time that muscles burn more fat for energy. If you want to stay lean without starving your body or working out to excess, you must add muscle.

As mentioned previously, bodybuilding was the spark that facilitated and developed the discipline, consistency, and commitment to health, fitness, physical, mental, and spiritual transformation. Bodybuilding is a sport that requires specific training and nutrition recommendations like most common professional sports. The sport is definitely not for everyone. The pathways to reducing excess body fat and achieving your physical transformation can definitely be achieved through the principles and weight training knowledge used in bodybuilding. These same scientific principles can be used in developing a fit and healthy body if done correctly. I recently saw a quote that stated, "It takes four weeks for you to notice your body changing, eight weeks for your friends to notice, and 12 weeks for the rest of the world to notice. Give yourself at least 12 weeks of consistent progress to start noticing the progress. Don't ever QUIT! You must keep moving forward.

I must emphasize having a coach or personal trainer does make a world of difference. During my off-season, my diet is typically clean 5-6 meals, and I don't believe in cheat meals. I usually follow a flexible meal plan, monitoring my macronutrients, not calories. I don't restrict myself from eating certain foods. I keep track of my macronutrient daily goals.

Macros are critical for determining how much carbohydrates, protein, and fat your body needs daily. These macros serve an important purpose when consumed into the body in a certain amount. Carbohydrates, for example, are broken down in the body to provide energy for the body to perform reactions and to regain stamina. Protein helps muscles to recover stronger than before, as well as help skin and hair cells to develop. Some substances, such as fat and micronutrients, can be beneficial for repairing and building immune responses in the body. These nutrients are vital to the human body, and without them, certain processes within the body can not take place. Proper diet and nutrition is a vital component to a long and healthy life.

I typically eat foods that meet my macronutrients goals year-round. Now, during Pre-contest prep, I am more strict with meal planning, and carbs intake is sometimes lower for different reasons. Carbs cycling has been extremely effective for helping me bring in a tighter and leaner physique. I haven't really experienced any failed diet plans in my competition meal prepping. My nutrients and calories usually fluctuate depending on how my body is progressing weekly towards each show for my bodybuilding competitions.

Below, you will find a simple meal plan and snacks I use for weight control with proper exercising. I use these plans not necessarily to lose weight but to reduce my body fat to achieve a leaner look. Remember, 80% of health is diet, and everyone has different body type caloric needs. Leaning out and gaining muscles is a science and specific method for each person. I am giving sample ideas on what to use to start out your journey. These ideas only sample clean methods you can use to start your health and fitness journey. Now, it has to become a lifestyle and do make modifications as needed based on physical and fitness goals.

I try to eat clean at least six days, and I have one cheat day. Again the equation is simple. Fewer calories in and more calories out if you want to lose weight (see picture in pervious paragraph). Anything else comes down to making healthy decisions. We all know those foods that we must give up to achieve our health goals. Also, you must watch your portions at all times. No matter what you are eating. Personally, I only eat from 8" or smaller plates while at home. I drink mainly water, IASO detox tea, no sodas, or juice. I drink the IASO teas to remove unhealthy pathogens from the intestinal track, repair bowel habits for boosting the immune system and metabolism. Other than that, water all day every day. Please visit::(https://befit4betterhealth.com/detox-tea-health-and-wellness-products) to learn more about this tea.

SAMPLE NUTRITION ~ CLEAN MEAL PLAN

DAY 1

BREAKFAST

1 1/2 Cup of Oatmeal

Three egg whites one whole egg

1 cup of IASO herbal tea

SNACK

4 oz of tuna and one plum or green apple

OR PROTEIN SHAKE

1 cup of IASO herbal tea

LUNCH

4oz of chicken/lean meat or turkey

1c of greens and one sweet potato

SNACK

Two scoops of protein/10 almonds

DINNER

5 oz of white fish or lean meat

2 c of VEGE

DAY 6   REPEAT MON-SAT

DAY7:   1 clean cheat meal

Sample Snacks List

1. One can Low Sodium V-8 100% Vegetable Juice

(30 calories, 1 gram of protein, 0 grams fat, 7 grams of carbohydrates, 1 gram dietary fiber, 80 mg sodium)

2. 14 Whole Natural Almonds

(80 calories, 3 grams of protein, 7 grams total fat, .5 grams saturated fat, 1.5 grams dietary fiber)

3. 1 Small box of raisins

(130 calories, 1 gram of protein, 0 grams total fat, 31 grams of carbohydrates, 2 grams dietary fiber)

4. Fruit, sliced and packed in plastic mini-bags, or whole

(Think apples, bananas, oranges, grapes, and more)

5. Sliced Veggies

(Cut them up and keep stored in the refrigerator, so they are ready to go. Think carrots and beyond such as sweet peppers, both green and red, broccoli, cauliflower, zucchini, snow peas, celery, cucumbers, fennel, and radishes. Calories vary, but you can eat a cup or so any of these for less than 100 calories.)

6. Babybel Light Cheese with 50 calories per piece.

7. Laughing Cow Light Cheese Wedge with 35 calories a wedge.

8. 3/4 cup Kashi Heart to Heart Cereal

(110 calories, 4 grams of protein, 1.5 grams total fat, 25 grams of carbohydrates, 5 grams dietary fiber. How about ½ cup Kashi Heart to Heart with 1 Tbsp. of either raisins or craisins for a total of about 100 calories. Makes a great low calorie, crunchy, and sweet trail mix.)

9. ¾ cup Quaker Crunchy Corn Bran

(90 calories with 5 grams of dietary fiber, 2 grams of protein, only 0.5 grams saturated fat)

10. ½ cup Quaker Oatmeal Squares

(105 calories with 2.5 grams of dietary fiber, 3 grams of protein, negligible saturated fat)

11. ½ of a Balance Bar

(Full bar has about 200 calories, 14 grams of protein, 6 grams of fat, 22 grams of carbohydrates)

12. ½ of a Larabar

These bars can be purchased 12 mini bars per box with a few hundred calories each. A variety of flavors are available, and they are made with very few ingredients. **A Jana Stewart Fitness favorite!!

13. 2 medium Kiwis

(90 calories or 45 calories each. Do watch how you transport these; they will bruise easily!)

14. 1 carton Vanilla Soy Milk

(120 calories, 7 grams of protein, 4 grams of total fat, 0.5 grams of saturated fat, 14 grams of carbohydrates, 2 grams of dietary fiber) **Great for mixing with just your Formula 1 Drink Mix.

15. 1 carton of low-fat plain or flavored Greek yogurt with 100 - 150 calories or less

16. Orville Redenbacher Smart Pop 94% Fat-free Butter Microwave Popcorn

(Has only 110 calories for a full mini-bag that makes about 6 cups of popcorn with 3 grams of protein, 0.5 grams of saturated fat, 4 grams of dietary fiber) **Watch out for Sodium

17. String cheese

(Look for convenient individual packages or larger packs in a variety of brands. For example, Reduced Fat, Low Moisture Mozzarella String Cheese by Sargento has 50 calories each, 6 grams of protein, 2.5 grams of total fat, 1.5 grams of saturated fat, 1 gram of carbohydrate)

18. Individual fruit cups

(70 calories, 1 gram of protein, 0 grams fat, 16 grams of carbohydrates, 1 gram of dietary fiber)

19. Organic Applesauce Cups

(Earth Kidz is one brand with 50 calories per cup, 0 grams protein, 0 grams fat, 13 grams carbohydrates, 1 gram dietary fiber.)

20. Pepperidge Farm whole-wheat mini bagels

(1 bagel has 100 calories, 4 grams of protein, 0.5 grams total fat, 20 grams of carbohydrates, 3 grams of dietary fiber)

21. Mi-Del Old-fashioned "Swedish Style" Vanilla Snaps

(These are all-natural, made with canola oil and have no trans fat. A serving size is five cookies with 130 calories, 4.5 grams of total fat, 21 grams of carbohydrates, and 1 gram of dietary fiber.)

22. Salmon Jerky

(1 package has 40 calories, 7 grams of protein, .5 grams fiber, 0 fat, 2 grams carbohydrate, 274 mg sodium. This product comes in various smoked flavors that are surprisingly good.

23. Reduced-Fat Triscuits by Nabisco

(A serving of 7 crackers has 120 calories with 3 grams of protein, 3 grams of total fat, 0 grams of saturated fat, 21 grams of carbohydrates, and 3 grams of dietary fiber.

24. Wasa Hearty Rye Crispbread

(45 calories per serving, 1 gram of protein, 0 grams of fat, 11 grams total carbohydrates, 2 grams of fiber)

25. Rice Cakes ~ Low Sodium plain

26. One Pomegranate

(100 calories, 1 gram of protein, 0 grams of fat, 26 grams of

carbohydrate, 1 gram of dietary fiber.)

Helping Tips for Building Muscle and Burning Fat

Year-round of competing for my health and fitness goals are very specific, which motivates me to remain consistent to train and fuel my body with purpose. My fitness journey has definitely kept me focused on maintaining my fitness and health process with maintaining muscle growth (mass) because muscles burn fat for energy to remain lean. I also utilized other methods such as intermittent fasting, detoxing, HIITs training to increase my metabolism rate by doing another weight lifting, cardio, and eating to fuel the body. As mentioned before, a huge part in mastering your health and fitness transformation will involve calculating your macros equal to your calorie intake, focus training for muscle growth, and doing other things outside of weight training such as intermittent fasting, HIIT, low and fast cardio to also help burn fat and Keeping it Simple and Sustainable and have a purpose and reason to my trainings.

Helpful Tips for Burning Fat

1. 1.Exercise to improve body composition and long-term results.
2. 2.Focus on building calorie-burning muscle mass,

then burning calories along.

3. 3.Replace the scale with monitoring body composition.

Cutting Out Sugar

The past two centuries, sugar has ruined peoples' bodies all over the world. The majority of the foods that we eat today have sugar in them, which could cause metabolic syndrome. The effect of metabolic syndrome in the human body is diabetes, health problems such as obesity in the system, which makes a human take more food than he or she is supposed to, and also could cause dental health issues such as the toothache. The effects that diabetes has on the body are bad circulation through the body, which could lead to death, high blood pressure, heart disease, and not excluding cancer.

Sugar addiction is a major stumbling block in an attempt to get people to change their behaviors. Sugar is found in everything and sometimes hidden in certain beverages that will not single out this information. People that drink and eat food high in sugar every day on average base has a very high percentage of getting diabetes. To stop this madness, people will have to slow down on drinking sodas, cookies, sweets, and sugar process foods. For example, look at organic food, healthiest things for your body, but it's so expensive which people will take the easy way out and buy sugary snacks and soda because it's cheaper. Now, slowing down on the amount of sugar that goes into the body on a weekly base and cutting down the big sodas will be a great health investment.

Now, cutting sugar out is not as easy as, but can start by stop adding three packets of processed sugar in your morning cup of coffee. Sugar is disguised in many different forms and is in a lot of ordinary food items you typically buy and wouldn't suspect it's in there. Sugars, labeled in one form or another, are added to a lot of foods that you would think are healthy. Yogurt, energy bars, ketchup, bread, crackers, salad dressings, and pasta sauce, to name a few. Read the labels. Sugar comes disguised under many different names. Be mindful of fruits consumed because certain fruits have a high amount of sugar, depending on the glycemic index of fruits. It can affect your weight loss goals. There are 61 different names for sugar. Usually, my clients are encouraged to do a 14-day challenge to start cutting sugar from the diet for better health benefits. Then they proceed to 21 days challenge. The goal of this challenege teaches people how to balance the amount of process sugar they're consuming on a consistent bases and becoming aware of different type of sugars in foods. As a result, my goal as a coach is helping people with eliminating these sugars from their eating habits gradually.

Some prevalent names for sugar to look for on the package ingredient list:

1. Sucrose
2. Maltose
3. Corn_Syrup
4. Agave_Nectar
5. Cane_Juice
6. Rice_Syrup
7. Barley_Malt
8. Beet_sugar
9. High_Fructose_Corn_Syrup
10. Molasses

Benefits of Reducing Sugar Intake are many and can Be Drastic:

Reducing sugar can create better weight management, which means less risk of obesity and related health effects. Significantly, decreased risk of type two diabetes means no daily insulin shots, no loss of feeling in extremities, and no daily blood testing. Reducing sugar intake lowers your risk for heart disease, currently the number one killer in the United States. Together, these health benefits paint a clear picture that reducing sugar intake has a significant health benefit and can possibly lead to a longer, more healthy life.

Detoxification for the Body

Detoxification is a process that involves flushing toxins harmful to the body, chemicals, and drugs out of your body. It's a normal body process of eliminating or neutralizing toxins through the colon, liver, kidneys, lungs, lymph glands, and skin. It may be done to remove metabolic wastes productions from eating and muscle products from training. The body needs to rid itself of the toxins that have built up in our fat stores throughout the years. Although your kidneys and liver are normally responsible for removing impurities, they need help sometimes. To keep your body running, your body goes through hundreds of metabolic functions every day. Over time, these metabolic functions will cause waste products to build up in your body. If left alone, these toxins can worsen current health issues and cause other medical problems.

During my off-season, I have learned detoxification can be a very important step toward living a healthy lifestyle. My method of detoxing is with Total Life Changer IASO tea wellness products. This tea is designed to remove waste from your body and cleanse your organs. The tea definitely has kept me feeling refueled and keeps my internal bowel habits, consistently moving toxins out daily.I have used in the past other teas, but definitely, this tea product has produced the desired results without abdominal pain, cramping, and experiences from other teas in the past. Some hot herbal tea early in the morning has been a great regime; it has helped with ensuring to start out my detox routine habit too.

Detoxing is a great way to get a head start on weight loss and learn how to have a healthy lifestyle. As long as you continue to follow healthy habits, you can enjoy having a sense of well-being that lasts. Over time, you may feel the impact of this improved well-being at work, in your relationships, and in your general outlook on life. When your body is not able to remove waste products efficiently, you need a good detoxification program to provide your liver with a boost.

Intermittent Fasting

There are many existing benefits of intermittent fasting for health benefits. I have used these methods to keep my overall body lean. There is much scientific evidence out there about fasting and its benefits to one's health. The evidence has shown many reasons to consider fasting as a benefit to your health.

Typically, the body heals itself and repairs all the damaged organs during a fast. There is good evidence to show that regulated fasting contributes to a longer life. It's also recommended to discuss with your doctors for fasting periods recommendations based on your healthcare conditions for the best time to fast. A fast does not chemically begin until the carbohydrate stores in the body begin to be used as an energy source. The fast will continue as long as fat and carbohydrate stores are used for energy, as opposed to protein stores. Once protein stores begin to be depleted for energy (resulting in loss of muscle mass), a person is technically starving. Therefore, be cautious, seek professional supervision, and guidance with fasting.

Sample Steps for Fasting

Before you start Intermittent Fasting, include some of these specific steps below

1) Pick the protocol that works with your lifestyle (explained further below): 16/8 Protocol: 16 hours of fasting, 8 hours of feasting every day. Example: eat your first meal at 12 pm, and stop eating by 8 pm each day…etc

24-hour fast Protocol: 24 hours of fasting 1x-2x per week normally eat otherwise.

2) Give your body time to adjust! You might feel hungry or tired at first; you've to train your body to expect food every 16 hours over time. This could take many days. Do this as a 1-month experiment. See how your body responds and adjusts along the way.

3) Drinking water, black coffee, or black/green tea during your fasted period is acceptable, but no liquid calories! Avoid all calories during fasting, and confine all eating to the "feasting" window.

4) Exercise during a fast for a turbo boost of fat loss. Fasted morning walks and strength training during the fasted window can help reduce body fat. If you get lightheaded, drink plenty of water. Make sure you are consuming enough calories during your 'feasting 8 hours' window to fuel your lifestyle.

5) Consume enough calories for your body type and goals. During your eating window, eat healthy sized meals that leave you full, and track your progress.

6) Start with 16/8 or 24-hour fasts, but adjust it to your schedule. Some people like 20/4 or 18/6. Or they do 24-hour fasts 2x per week instead of once. Make it work for your life.

7) Combine this with other strategies for maximum

effectiveness. Intermittent Fasting can be combined with exercise, a nutritious diet composed of vegetables, protein, and healthy fats, and plenty of sleep.

CHAPTER SIX

Get Fit with Health Coaching

"Every day is another chance to get stronger, to eat better, to live healthier, and to be the best version of you."

I want you to think about a moment, and you were "told" by your healthcare provider or clinician to eat healthier to improve your health. Perhaps a family or even a good friend probably has told you to eat healthier meals to improve your overall health.

Well, over the years, there is an emerging approach for improving an individual's health. This approach is known as coaching. It's a different pathway from the traditional way of being told to be healthier. The term coaching can be seen as empowering an individual to be at the center of their health care decisions. Coaching is goal-oriented, client-centered partnership, health-focused, and filled with enlightenment and empowerment to achieving personal health and fitness goals. You being the client at your doctor's office receiving care, how would that approach make you feel, think about it, and compare it to being "told" to do something without appropriate guidance.

The vast majority of diseases, disability, and healthcare costs are contributed by chronic illness. These illnesses include high blood pressure, diabetes, obesity, and cancer. The common risk factors associated with these illnesses are often link to a lack of physical activity and nutrition. The national trends show 64% of adults are overweight, approximately 30% of adults are obese, 17% of children ages 6-18 are overweight. Obesity is the second leading cause of unnecessary deaths. Consumers spend $33 billion a year on the diet industry. Every year, about 8 million people sign up for weight loss programs that offer a quick result solution. Having a health or fitness coach can help you figure out how much cardio and weight training you need or figure out the best cardio that works for your time and makes fitness enjoyable for you. My coach Stephanie truly helped me in balancing my fitness life without becoming consumed with fitness competitions.

Coaching has shown through the evidence base research as a method to improve nutrition habits, diabetes, physical activity, and many other healthcare outcomes.

My doctored equality improvement researched project at Florida Atlantic University focused on "The Effects of Diet of Diet Coaching and Nutrition Education on Protein Intake in Adults." The participants' in the coaching study showed clients' protein intakes were below the standard for protein recommendations. After ten weeks of diet coaching and nutrition education, participants' protein intake tripled per meal at breakfast, lunch, and dinner from baseline, five weeks, and ten weeks. The results shown from the diet coaching interaction with participants showed the significant impact coaching had on improving persons eating habits. Now, imagine the future of coaching approach for improving nutrition habits and health behaviors that can resolve chronic illness associated with nutrition. This evidence-based approach is becoming the pathway to improve the future healthcare of our nation.

To manage the problems associated with chronic illness, it's going to require people taking serious strong steps in managing and preventing chronic illness. One main reason for the increased prevalence of chronic health conditions is obesity. Being involved with a clinic focused on health coaching models will help you with your health changes strategies for healthier diets and increasing physical activities. This could result in lowering chronic diseases.

Some people with chronic and complex health conditions, especially those with multiple or severe chronic conditions, acquire a large proportion of spending in the health care system. In healthcare, Obesity has become a very serious problem affecting many Americans currently, and it's a problem that continues to grow each year. This issue has known to be the cause of many other chronic diseases such as diabetes type II, hyperlipidemia, and heart diseases. Implementing a cost-containment mechanism, emphasizing patient behavior-management educations, and evidence-based guidelines for weight loss and physical activity may help to control costs for those patients while improving or maintaining quality.

Health coaching and training can help people with depression to build self-esteem and create a sense of empowerment for patients in the community. Also, help you develop healthy fitness and nutrition behavior habits that will get you out of the vicious cycle of unhealthy habits. It provides a systematic method for healthcare, fitness, and wellness for people in making the positive lifestyle changes they need in order to increase health and well being. Integrating health and fitness single or group coaching will improve overall wellness.

A person with good health and fitness coaching becomes capable of living his/her life to its fullest extent. It is very important for a person in life to be physically and mentally fit to live a healthy and happy life. Health and fit people become less prone to medical conditions. Fitness does not mean to be physically fit only; it also means a healthy mental state of the person. One can get a healthy mental state if he/she becomes physically fit. The simple way to remain healthy and fit has stress free mind with regular exercise and a balanced diet. People who maintain their ideal weight become less prone to cardiac and other health problems. People who are physically active can easily maintain a relaxed state of mind. Healthy and fit people can easily face all the ups and downs of their life and less affected by any drastic change.

People are more conscious of their health and fitness as time changes. Male wants to have a muscle-bound body, whereas females want a slim and trim look. Everybody is doing lots of struggle on a daily basis to achieve a perfect body. Getting a healthy and fit body and mind requires lots of patience, time, commitment, goal, belief, and a strong mind to face all the struggles. Some people have the ability to maintain fitness on their own; however, some need a good qualified personal trainer to take care of the daily exercises and diet. People who are in corporate businesses have very little movement and a lot of sitting all through the day. That's why they face being overweight, obese, lazy, and tired. It is proved with studies that people who are more fit and healthy achieve greater success in life.

Nowadays, people have been so busy with their hectic lifestyle and do not have time to keep themselves healthy or stay fit. It is the fact that we must eat healthy, practice cleanliness, and involve in daily physical exercises in order to remain healthy and fit. As we know that there is no alternative to hard work, in the same way, there is no alternative to health and fitness. Health and fitness is a combination of healthy living with a healthy lifestyle. Psychological health is very necessary for the physical health of a person in order to be healthy and fit. We need to eat healthy food and do physical exercises on a daily basis in order to remain physically healthy; however, we need to think positive to remain mentally healthy.

We need to get self-motivated as well as take part in the fitness-style activities. We should take our fitness as a matter of every-day routine. Being fit should be our first aim in living a healthy lifestyle. It doesn't require exercising for hours; just a small amount of exercise and healthy food on a daily basis is enough to maintain health and fitness. We should keep our eyes always open and select stairs instead of the elevator, use cycle instead of car or bike for nearby areas, walk to the next bus stop, etc. It really creates a big difference. Being involved in daily physical exercises not only keeps us fit, but also improve our lifestyle and healthy living. It increases our energy level and thus confidence level.

CHAPTER SEVEN

Creating Your Training Plan

"Action is the foundational key to all success." — Pablo Picasso,

You have arrived at the final chapter in this book. I hope by now, you have found some important health and fitness information that will move you into actions towards your own journey for better health. This chapter has a few examples of some action plans filled with outline physical activity to get you going on your fitness journey. Investing time into you will the best investment you'll ever make towards your health and fitness goals. You're worth it! There is no better time than now to start walking down the path to better health and a sense of self-worth. You can start by improving your exercising training habits, eating habits, and quality time you spend with yourself. The choice start with you, but you have to be willing to be committed and be disciple through the process. Even small amounts of exercise are better than none at all. Start with an activity you enjoy and can do comfortably. As you become used to exercising, try to exercise within your target heart rate zone so that you get the most benefit.

Getting Started Resistance Training Sample

You should be exercising 3- 6 days a week, with one day of rest. Please do not exercise on a rest day, as it will compromise your body's ability to heal itself.

Resistance Training:

Gain muscle: Each exercise do 3-4 sets, 12-15 reps

Lean out: Each exercise does 4-5 sets, 12-15 reps

Chest and back- 1-2x a week

Shoulders/biceps/triceps- 1-2x a week

Legs and glutes-3x a week

Abs- every other day

Rest: one day per week

*Note: Resistance training should last approx 30-60 minutes each day

Cardio Training:

Gain muscle (men): Cardio 3x a week 30 minutes

Gain muscle (women): 4-5x a week 30 min

Lean out: Cardio: 5-6x a week 45 min

Rest: one day per week

Cardio suggestions:

Interval training

Treadmill incline

Stadiums

Elliptical

Stairclimber

Rotating Stairmill

Weight Training Sample Plan

MONDAY - (UPPER BODY):

Warm-Up- Jog on a treadmill for about 10-mins to get the heart rate up

Dumbbell Hammer Curls- 3 sets of 15 reps

Dumbbell Curls- 3 sets of 15 reps

Dumbbell shoulder press- 3 sets of 15 reps

Lateral Raises- 3 sets of 15

Triceps Kickback- 3 sets of 15

Cardio: 30 minutes (treadmill incline 10-15 speed 2.0-4.0, stair masters, cycling, walking, running outdoors or indoors and swimming).

TUESDAY-

REST DAY:

WEDNESDAY- (GLUTES/LEGS):

Warm-Up- Jog on a treadmill for about 10 mins.to get the heart rate up.

Dumbbell Squats- 4 sets of 20 reps.

Walking Lunges -(use 5-15lbs dumbbell) 4 sets of 20 steps

Sumo Squats Dumbbells- 4 sets of 20 reps.

Donkey Kickback- 4 sets of 15 reps each leg.

-Stretch

**Bonus Challenge! "Wall Sits" for 1 min!!

THURSDAY-
REST DAY

FRIDAY-(ABS/CARDIO)

Jump Rope- 3 sets for 1 min

Crunches- 3 sets of 20 reps

Knee/Leg Raises- 3 sets of 20 reps

Weight Russian Twist- Complete 20x 4 (use plate)

Jump Rope- 3 sets for 1 min

Plank- holds for 1 min x3 total 3 minutes

Cardio: 30 minutes

SATURDAY -(GLUTES/LEGS)

Warm-Up- Jog on a treadmill for about 10-mins.to get the

heart rate up

- Leg Extensions- 3 sets of 15 reps
- Walking Lunges -(use 10-15lbs dumbbell) 3 sets of 12 reps
- Leg Press- (Moderate weight)
- Three sets of 15 reps with feet wider
- -Stretch
- **Bonus Challenge! "Wall Sits" for 1 min!!

SUNDAY-

REST DAY, Make sure to stretch your entire body

Visual Pictures Weight Training

Dumbbells Shoulder Press 5lbs, 15 Reps x 4 sets

Dumbbell Shoulder Press

Dumbbells Lateral Raises 5lbs, 15 reps x 4 sets

Dumbbell Lateral Raise (Power Partials)

Walking Lunges with Dumbbells 5lbs 20 steps x 4 sets

Dumbbell Lunges

Sumo Squads with 15-20lbs Dumbbells 20 Reps x 4 sets

Crunches 100 (25 Reps x 4 Sets)

Wall Sit / Squat

Donkey Kicks

Hammer Curls

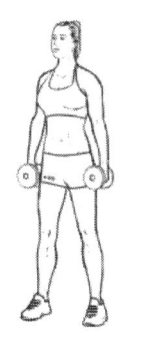

Tricep Dumbbell Kickback

Beginners Guides to Go from

Walking to Running 5k

I heard many people often say "I cannot run a 5k" today, I am here to provide you with some simple steps to help you on your journey to walk or run your 5k race or even improve your fitness goals. Many people may have known me as a bodybuilder, but I am naturally a born running athlete from the heart. Before learning about bodybuilding and acquiring knowledge on weighting lifting, running was the foundation that kept my health and body in the best shape. If I didn't walk away from running a dream in high school, I always believed I would have been an Olympic gold medalist track athlete. Running and even walking can tremendously improve your life, health, and make you happier.

When you start your walk and run routines, make sure you take time to listen to your body. Work at a pace that's comfortable for your fitness level, but make sure to put in the necessary effort – just don't overdo it. Stretch before and after every workout session. If you want to make sure you're also burning off some fat while you're at it, during the running phase of each workout, make sure you keep it at a moderate intensity level. That's generally about 60-70% of your maximum heart rate. I also recommend you visit a running shoe store to purchase good running shoes with some good insoles. Trust and listen to your body, your knees will definitely appreciate it. Remember, after each run, recover with stretching, warm Epsom baths, and messages as needed. Now, go on and register for your 5k race. Now on to your 5k run or walk challenge... BEST Wishes!

RUN/WALK FOR BETTER HEALTH 5K GUIDE

Week 1:

5 minutes warm-up walk 10-minute brisk walk, 10-minute walk (Finsih cool down)

* (Repeat walk or running routine three times per week, example Monday, Wednesday, and Saturday).

Week 2:

5 minutes warm-up walk, 15-minutes brisk walk or jogging, 10-minute walk cool down.

(Repeat 3 times per week, example Monday, Wednesday, and Saturday).

Week 3:

5 minutes warm-up walk 20-minute brisk walk, 5-minute jog, 5-minutes walks

(Repeat 3 times per week, example Monday, Wednesday, and Saturday).

Week 4:

5 minutes warm-up walk, 10-minute jog and walk, 10-minute walk

(Repeat 3 times per week, example Monday, Wednesday, and Saturday).

Week 5:

5 minutes warm-up walk, 15-minute jog and walk, 10-minute walk

(Repeat 4 times per week, example Monday, Wednesday, Friday and Saturday).

Week 6:

5 minutes warm-up walk, 20-minute jog and walk, 10-minute walk

(Repeat 4 times per week, example Monday, Wednesday, Friday, and Saturday).

Week 7:

5 minutes warm-up walk, 10-minute jog, and run, 10-minute walk

(Repeat 4 times per week, example Monday, Wednesday, Fridays and Saturday).

Week 8:

5 minutes warm-up walk, 15-minute jog, and run, 10-minute walk

(Repeat 3 times per week, example Monday, Wednesday, and Saturday).

Week 9:

5 minutes warm-up walk, 20-minute jog, or run, 10-minute walk

(Repeat 3 times per week, example Monday, Wednesday, and Saturday).

Week 10:

5 minutes warm-up walk, 30-minute jog, or run, 10-minute walk

(Repeat 3 times per week, example Monday, Wednesday, and Saturday).

CONGRATULATIONS!!! REMEMBER TO REWARD YOURSELF AFTER COMPLETING THE 10 WEEKS RUN WALK PROGRAM.

CONCLUSION

I hope as you venture on a fitness journey and continue the pathway to befit for better health. Focus on becoming more aware of the points mention on how to keep healthy both physically and mentally. Some people know well about how to keep their body neat, clean, and healthy; however, they carry stresses in their mind, so they always lack the motivation to be consistent with health and fitness goals. Mental stress gradually deteriorates the good condition of the body and makes it weak and prone to diseases. People who are serious about their health and fitness do exercises on a daily basis and eat healthy food in a timely manner. They are much conscious about their health and avoid being lazy, eating unhealthy food, and sedentary life. We should aim to enjoy spending time in the morning meditating, praying, walking, running, working out at the gym, or other physical activities to keep our spirit and soul balanced and body functioning well to improve overall health and fitness benefits.

We should aim to eat freshly cooked food instead of processed foods on consistent bases in order to remain away from the digestive and health disorders. It helps to construct our minds and motivate your to take control, ownership, and responsibility of our total body wellbeing. As chronic health problems and generally unhealthy life choices increase, a dark shadow is generated over the life that prevents many people from living an enjoyable healthy life. The unfortunate health outcomes of living an unhealthy life and illness extinguish our natural light, keeps real joy at arm's length, and undermines the self-love and confidence that sustains us. Use your LIGHT to strive to live a balanced life composed of fitness; develop your personal self-worth through hard work, setting attainable goals, and positive reinforcement. This approach to total body wellbeing will help many to Shine and live a healthy and vibrant life. Regardless of what stage you're currently in with your health & fitness goals. You can build the confidence to live in a brand new light-filled with energy, self-love, and living confidence with a positive self-image for better health. I am extremely grateful to wake up everyday living a life towards fitness for better health. This fitness and healthy lifestyles require your time, energy, and committed towards being fully conscious about healthy choices you make consistently on a daily basis towards being fit for better health.

About the Author

Dr. Maude Exantus is a Doctorate-prepared Family Nurse Practitioner, Certified Health Coach, Clinical Educator Faculty, Nutrition Consultant, IFBB Figure Pro athlete, and founder of Befit 4 Better Health and owner of LightShine Health & Fitness LLC, a professional consultancy business dedicated to health, fitness and wellness for people in all aspects of life. She has over 16 years of experience in the healthcare industry. Maude received her Bachelor's and Master's Degree in Nursing from Barry University and went on to earn her Doctor in Nursing Practice DNP degree, focused on coaching and nutrition education at Florida Atlantic University. Maude has participated in various areas of fitness events, including bodybuilding competitions, marathon races, Crossfit, and instructor for group fitness exercises classes.

These various experiences and exposures have led Maude

into the pathway of pursuing her passion for transforming the culture of healthcare, through fitness with various strategic approaches to wellness. Maude is passionate about inspiring people to increase physical fitness levels for building optimum health. Maude's personal fitness transformation for better health lead her to create awareness to improve people's health concerns through "BeFit 4 Better Health," using her health and fitness expertise knowledge to transform others into healthier and more vibrant beings.

Dr. Maude Exantus' mission is focused on changing the culture of how health, fitness, and wellness management in primary care practice and communities. Her long-term goal is devoted to communities and people seeking motivation and additional knowledge about maintaining great health and fitness conditioning. Maude demonstrates and maintains her health and fitness lifestyle by competing as a figure competitor with proper and balanced nutrition with hard work in the gym to inspire others towards claiming their personal health fitness and wellness lifestyle. Only 5 percent of people in this world can achieve or tolerate the level of discipline required as a competitor. Her fitness journey has given her knowledge and lessons required to help others master their own health and fitness transformations. Competing has given her more discipline, commitment, and consistency with maintaining motivation and accountability towards her nutrition and fitness training workouts.

BeFIT4 BETTER HEALTH NOTES

Made in the USA
Columbia, SC
09 June 2020